2010 FIFA WORLD CUP

SOUTH AFRICA™

FACT FILE

Contents

© 2007 FIFA TM

Introduction

There's no event quite like the FIFA World Cup™. Since it began in 1930, it has grown into the single biggest sporting spectacle on the planet.

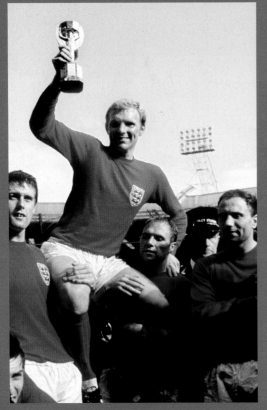

England celebrate winning the FIFA World Cup™ in 1966.

For one month every four years, football is all anyone anywhere will be talking about. In every country, on every continent, there will be endless discussion and heated debate about the competition. Why? Because football remains the game, the universal language, that unites nations across the globe.

At the last FIFA World Cup™ in Germany in 2006, a total of over 26 billion people around the world watched the tournament on television, culminating in that memorable final between Italy and France in Berlin.

Diego Maradona lead Argentina to FIFA World Cup™ triumph in 1986.

France's Didier Deschamps lifting the FIFA World Cup™ in 1998.

Four years on and the world is once more waiting for the big event, especially as it will be the first time that the FIFA World Cup™ has been held in Africa.

One thing is for sure – it's going to be an amazing tournament, with the greatest players in the world, showing their skills on the biggest stage of all. There will be passion and pride. There will be heroes and villains. There will be laughter and tears. There will be success and heartbreak.

The whole world will be watching...

Italy won the 2006 FIFA World Cup™ defeating France in the final.

Meet Zakumi

From World Cup Willie in 1966 to Goleo and Pille in Germany in 2006, the FIFA World Cup™ Official Mascot has long been a key player in any FIFA World Cup™ tournament. They don't just put a smile on people's faces, but play a big role in helping to bring the football world together, regardless of any language barriers.

This time, the task has been given to Zakumi – 2010 FIFA World Cup South Africa™ Official Mascot. Fresh, friendly and fun, Zakumi's been hard at work since he was unveiled in September 2008, travelling all over Africa, making friends and inviting everyone along to the FIFA World Cup™ party in South Africa in 2010.

SOUTH AFRICA 2010

1 Zakumi was born on June 16, 1994 – the same day as Youth Day in South Africa.

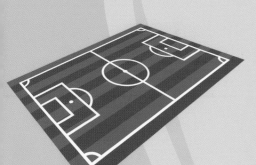

2 Zakumi's name comes from "ZA" which is the code for South Africa and "kumi" which translates as 'ten' in various languages across Africa.

4 Zakumi's green and gold colours are the same as those used in South Africa's flag.

3 Zakumi dyed his hair green to camoflage himself on the football field!

"Zakumi wants to create a good mood for the fans and raise the excitement for the 2010 FIFA World Cup™, the first on African soil," says the South African football icon Lucas Radebe. "He is a proud South African and wants to ensure that the world will come together in South Africa."

5 Zakumi's want's to turn the 2010 FIFA World Cup South Africa™ into one huge, joyful and unforgettable party and show the thousands of international guests the warmth and spirit of the African continent.

Welcome to South Africa

Since the end of the apartheid regime in 1994, South Africa and its people have worked together to create a modern, vibrant nation that embraces diversity and welcomes the rest of the world. A country with over 47 million people spanning nine provinces, it has a rich variety of languages, cultures, beliefs and histories.

From vast, open plains to modern, bustling cities, South Africa has something for everyone. There's wildlife and spectacular mountains, the world-famous Kruger National Park and fantastic beaches galore. And, of course, there are its people. Drawn from vastly different backgrounds and with 11 official national languages – Zulus and Swazi, Tsonga and Venda, Sotho and Afrikaans – to name but a few. Archbishop Desmond Tutu once described the country as the "Rainbow Nation" and it's easy to see why. But while it may be diverse, there is one thing that unites pretty much everyone and that's sport. In fact, sport is not so much a hobby in South Africa as a religion, and this summer, when the 19th FIFA World Cup™ kicks off at Soccer City in Johannesburg, you're going to see the nation's passion for sport in an abundance.

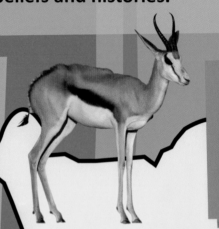

The country's national animal is the springbok, which also gives its name to the South African rugby team – they're known as "The Boks".

South African fans are some of the best in the world.

The national sports of South Africa are rugby union and cricket, followed by football.

Cape Town

South Africa has a rich variety of indigenous animals. From elephants to lions, rhinos to giraffes, there are over 200 species of mammals in the country.

Polokwane

Nelspruit

South Africa covers over 1.2 million square kilometres – that's bigger than Texas and California put together!

Rustenburg

Pretoria

Johannesburg

Soccer City stadium, Johannesburg.

Johannesburg is the largest city in South Africa with a population of over 7 million.

The South African national team's nickname is Bafana Bafana which translates as "The Boys, The Boys".

Bloemfontein

Durban

There are 11 official languages in South Africa, including Zulu, Xhosa and English.

South Africa is the world's second biggest gold producer. It's also responsible for around 15 per cent of the world's diamonds.

The South African Premier League has 16 teams. The current champions are Supersport United from Pretoria.

Port Elizabeth

Tour the Stadiums

South Africa is a nation obsessed with sport. From football to cricket, rugby to athletics, they just can't get enough of it. It's hardly surprising then that they have some of the best stadiums in the world. Ever since FIFA President Sepp Blatter announced South Africa as host nation for the 2010 World Cup South Africa™ Finals in May 2004, there's been lots of building work carried out across the country in preparation.

Some stadiums, like the Free State Stadium in Bloemfontein or the Rustenburg's Royal Bafokeng Stadium have been upgraded or expanded, whilst elsewhere, like at Polokwane and Durban, new, state-of-the-art stadiums have been built from scratch. There are now ten world class venues ready, willing and more than capable of hosting the world's biggest sporting event, and in Johannesburg's giant 94,000-capacity Soccer City, home to the final itself, South Africa has a venue as good as any sports stadium in the world. The scene is set for a truly memorable month of world class football...

Construction: *New – completed 2009*
Pitch Size: *105m x 68m*
Capacity: *46,000*

Mbombela Stadium, *Nelspruit*

A new ground and the first international standard stadium in the Mpumalanga Province. With a capacity of 46,000, the name "Mbombela" literally means "many people together in a small space".

Free State Stadium, *Bloemfontein*

The home of South African Premier League soccer side Bloemfontein Celtics, the Free State Stadium was also one of the venues for the 2009 FIFA Confederations Cup. For the FIFA World Cup™ Finals a new second tier has been added to the main stand, taking the total capacity to 48,000.

Construction: *Built 1952 – upgraded 2009*
Pitch Size: *105m x 68m*
Capacity: *48,000*

Nelson Mandela Bay Stadium, *Port Elizabeth*

Construction: *New – completed 2009*
Pitch Size: *105m x 68m*
Capacity: *48,000*

With its unique position on the shores of the North End Lake, the new Nelson Mandela Bay Stadium is one of the most spectacular stadiums on show at the 2010 FIFA World Cup South Africa™ Finals. A total of eight games will be played at the stadium, including a quarter-final and the third and fourth place play-off.

Royal Bafokeng Stadium, *Rustenburg*

Construction: *Built 1999 – minor upgrade 2010*
Pitch Size: *105m x 68m*
Capacity: *48,000*

Originally a rugby stadium, this ground as undergone a revamp for the 2010 FIFA World Cup™ Finals and now boasts an extra 4,000 seats, new hi-tech electronic scoreboards and a cool new lighting system.

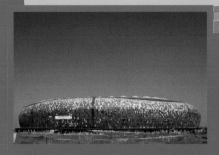

Construction: *Built 1987 – major upgrade 2009*
Pitch Size: *105m x 68m*
Capacity: *94,700*

Soccer City Stadium, *Johannesburg*

Designed to look like an African pot called a "calabash" the new look Soccer City has the third largest capacity of any stadium in the whole of Africa and will make a fitting home for the 2010 FIFA World Cup South Africa™ Final.

Construction: *New – completed 2010*
Pitch Size: *105m x 68m*
Capacity: *46,000*

Peter Mokaba Stadium, *Polokwane*

One of five new venues being built for the Finals, the 46,000 capacity Peter Mokaba Stadium is situated in Polokwane, the capital of the Limpopo Province and will host four group matches.

Construction: *Built 1982 – minor upgrade 2009*
Pitch Size: *105m x 68m*
Capacity: *62,000*

Ellis Park Stadium, *Johannesburg*

The scene of South Africa's rugby World Cup win in 1995, Ellis Park holds a special place in the hearts of South African sports fans. The home of Orlando Pirates FC, it now has a new tier on the North Stand taking its capacity to an impressive 62,000.

Green Point Stadium, *Cape Town*

A stone's throw from the ocean and in the shadow of the famous Table Mountain, the new 70,000 seater Green Point Stadium is set in one of the most idyllic locations of all the FIFA World Cup™ venues. It will host five first round matches, one second round match, one quarter-final and one semi-final.

Construction: *New – completed 2009*
Pitch Size: *105m x 68m*
Capacity: *68,000*

Construction: *New – completed 2009*
Pitch Size: *105m x 68m*
Capacity: *70,000*

Moses Mabhida Stadium, *Durban*

With its huge arch towering over 100 metres above this new stadium, the Moses Mabhida Stadium is destined to become one of the most recognizable venues at the 2010 FIFA World Cup South Africa™. The 70,000 seat arena was built on the site of the old Kings Park Stadium.

Construction: *Built 1906 – minor upgrade 2008*
Pitch Size: *105m x 68m*
Capacity: *50,000*

Loftus Versfeld Stadium, *Pretoria*

One of the oldest stadiums in South Africa, the Loftus Versfeld was the site of South Africa's first-ever win over a European international team in 1999 when they defeated Sweden 1-0. It will host five group matches and one second round match.

© 2007 FIFA TM

Ten Amazing FIFA World Cup™ Facts

607,900,000

The number of people around the world that watched the 2006 FIFA World Cup™ final between France and Italy on television.

199,854

The estimated number of fans that crammed into Rio de Janeiro's Maracana Stadium for the 1950 FIFA World Cup™ finale between Brazil and Uruguay.

11 The number of seconds it took Turkey's Hakan Sukur to score the fastest goal in FIFA World Cup™ history against South Korea in 2002.

17 At 17 years and 41 days, Northern Ireland's Norman Whiteside became the youngest ever player at the FIFA World Cup™ Finals when he played against Yugoslavia in 1982.

The weight in grams of the solid gold FIFA World Cup™ Trophy – about the same as two average-sized newborn babies.

6,174

15 The number of FIFA World Cup™ goals scored by Ronaldo – he was a member of the Brazil squad in 1994, 1998, 2002 and 2006.

The number of sausages consumed by football fans during the last FIFA World Cup™ Finals in Germany in 2006.

3,500,000

56 How many seconds it took Uruguay's Jose Batista to get sent off against Scotland in 1986.

1 The number of players who have scored at both ends in the same FIFA World Cup™ Finals match. The unlucky man was Holland's Ernie Brandts against Italy in 1978.

27 The number of goals scored by Hungary in the 1954 Finals – the highest total in FIFA World Cup™ history.

Thirty-two teams will descend on South Africa to compete for the biggest prize in world football and there's some truly mouth-watering games in prospect.

The festival of football will kick off in Johannesburg when the hosts South Africa take on Mexico, followed soon after by Uruguay versus France in Cape Town. In Group B, meanwhile, two–time champions Argentina take on Nigeria, with South Korea and Greece filling the other places. Group C sees Fabio Capello's England facing the USA, Algeria and Slovenia, with Group D boasting Germany, Serbia, Ghana and Australia. The Netherlands has been paired with Japan, Cameroon and the rapidly improving Denmark while the current holders Italy begin the defence of their title in Group F against Paraguay, Slovakia and New Zealand. Group G would appear to be one of the toughest with Brazil, Portugal, North Korea and the Ivory Coast all squaring up, while reigning European champions Spain will have to play Chile, Switzerland and Honduras.

The countdown to the 2010 FIFA World Cup South Africa™ truly began once the first round group matches were announced.

In short, there's going to be a lot of football in South Africa this summer. It's going to be fascinating. It's going to be frenetic.

It's going to be a whole lot of fun....

Group A:
South Africa
Mexico
Uruguay
France

Group B:
Argentina
Nigeria
South Korea
Greece

Group C:
England
United States
Algeria
Slovenia

Group D:
Germany
Australia
Serbia
Ghana

Group E:
Netherlands
Denmark
Japan
Cameroon

Group F:
Italy
Paraguay
New Zealand
Slovakia

Group G:
Brazil
North Korea
Côte d'Ivoire
Portugal

Group H:
Spain
Switzerland
Honduras
Chile

COMPLETE THE 2010 FIFA WORLD CUP SOUTH AFRICA™ PROGRESS CHART ON PAGES 62–63.

South Africa GROUP A

Traditionally, the host nations at a FIFA World Cup™ Finals always seem to rise to the occasion. Can South Africa do the same in 2010?

FIFA World Cup™ Record

The South African national team was only allowed back into international football following the end of apartheid in 1990 but it would be eight years before they made their first appearance in the FIFA World Cup™ Finals when they qualified for the tournament in France. But, like their second showing four years later in Japan and South Korea, it ended in a first round exit. This time around, they'll be hoping to do much better.

FIFA World Cups™
Hosted: *1 - 2010*

Best FIFA World Cup™
Finish: *First Round – 1998, 2002*

How They Qualified

As the host nation, South Africa were spared the test of a qualifying campaign, instead using competitions like the 2009 Confederations Cup to test their mettle against strong international teams.

Manager: Carlos Alberto Parreira

Having resigned for personal reasons in 2008, Carlos Alberto Parriera returned as coach of South Africa, replacing Joel Santana. Certainly, here is a manager who can make things happen – he has coached at five different FIFA World Cup™ Finals, with four different countries, and led his home nation, Brazil, to glory in 1994.

Key Man: Bernard Parker

Since his call up to the national side in 2007, Parker has more than proved he has what it takes in international football, scoring goals freely and suggesting that he could be the man to eclipse Benni McCarthy's record tally of goals for South Africa.

Mexico

With a clutch of new talent coming through the ranks and an expectant set of supporters, could this be Mexico's year?

> **FIFA World Cups™**
> **Hosted:** *2 – 1970, 1986*
> **Best FIFA World Cup™ Finish:**
> *Quarter-finals – 1970, 1986*

FIFA World Cup™ Record

Though they have hosted two of the most memorable tournaments in FIFA World Cup™ history, Mexico has yet to really make a mark at the Finals. In 12 appearances they have never gone further than the quarter-finals, in 1970 and 1986.

How They Qualified

What looked like being a disastrous qualifying campaign for Mexico eventually turned into an incredible comeback. A 3-1 loss to Honduras left their place in doubt and Swedish coach Sven-Goran Eriksson was replaced with Javier Aguirre. The transformation was completed in October 2009 when, in front of 100,000 spectators at the Estadio Azteca, they defeated El Salvador 4-1. It sealed a quite amazing turnaround in their fortunes.

Key Man: Andres Guardado

With a fearsome left-foot and pace to spare, Andres Guardado is a vital cog in Javier Aguirre's attacking options. A left-winger who now plays his club football for Deportivo La Coruna in Spain's La Liga, he will be charged with providing the ammunition for the likes of Miguel Sabah and Carlos Vela upfront.

Manager: Javier Aguirre

Aguirre stepped in to take charge after the short-lived reign of Sven-Goran Eriksson. Now in his second stint as national coach – he was first manager in 2001–2002 – Aguirre has steadied the ship and, remarkably, turned Mexico's perilous qualifying position into an automatic place.

Uruguay

GROUP A

After missing out in 2006, the winners of the very first FIFA World Cup™ are back again...

FIFA World Cups™ Hosted: *1 – 1930*
FIFA World Cup™ Won: *2 – 1930, 1950*

FIFA World Cup™ Record

Winners of the inaugural FIFA World Cup™ in 1930, Uruguay repeated the feat in 1950 when they defeated hosts Brazil at the Maracana Stadium. With a population of just over 3 million, they remain the smallest country to ever win the tournament.

How They Qualified

Uruguay was the last team to qualify for the 2010 FIFA World Cup™ Finals. Having secured fifth place in the South American zone of qualifying, a narrow 2-1 victory over two legs in the play-off against Costa Rica won their spot.

The Manager: Oscar Tabarez

Now his second stint in charge of the national team, Tabarez managed 'La Celeste' or 'the Sky Blues' during the FIFA World Cup™ Finals in Italy in 1990 where they reached the last 16. Tabarez has also managed some of the biggest club sides in world football, including AC Milan in Italy and Boca Juniors in Argentina.

Key Man: Diego Forlan

Striker Diego Forlan hails from a footballing family – his father played for Uruguay in the 1966 FIFA World Cup™ – and, despite an unsuccessful spell at Manchester United from 2002–2004, Forlan has gone on to great things, first at Villarreal and currently at Atletico Madrid. In 2009, he won the European Golden Boot for the most goals scored in the season.

20

France

It's been 12 years since France won the FIFA World Cup™, but are they in a position to do it again in 2010?

FIFA World Cup™ Record

For a nation with such a proud tradition in the game, it took a very long time for France to claim the FIFA World Cup™ title. But after ten attempts, they finally triumphed on home soil in 1998 when they famously beat Brazil 3-0, prompting jubilant scenes across France.

> FIFA World Cups™
> Hosted : *2 – 1938, 1998*
> FIFA World Cup™ Won:
> *1 – 1998*

How They Qualified

Having finished second to Serbia in UEFA Group 7, Raymond Domenech's side faced a difficult play-off against the Republic of Ireland. It would be a tight contest, with 'Les Bleus' advancing thanks to a controversial late goal from William Gallas.

The Manager: Raymond Domenech

The surprise choice to replace Jacques Santini after France's exit from the Euro 2004, Domenech was previously the coach of the French Under-21 side and also gained eight caps for his country in the 1970s. In 2006, he guided the French side to runners-up spot in the FIFA World Cup™ Finals in Germany.

Key Man: Franck Ribery

Pursued by some of the biggest clubs in European football, Ribery came burst onto the scene in the 2006 FIFA World Cup™ Finals. Since then, the Bayern Munich winger has matured into one of the best attacking wide men in the game, attracting interest from the likes of Real Madrid and Chelsea.

Argentina

One of the true superpowers in world football, Argentina has the skill, guile and experience to go very far in 2010...

FIFA World Cups™
Hosted: *1 – 1978*
FIFA World Cups™ Won:
2 – 1978, 1986

FIFA World Cup™ Record

Having lived in the shadow of their South American rivals and neighbours, Brazil, Argentina finally came of age in the 1970s taking the title on home soil after a memorable 3-1 victory over The Netherlands. Eight years later in Mexico, inspired by the genius of Diego Maradona, they took the title for a second time, defeating West Germany 3-2 in the final at the Estadio Azteca.

How They Qualified

Unusually for Argentina, qualification for the Finals in South Africa was not a foregone conclusion. In their last game against Uruguay they needed a win to claim the fourth and final automatic qualification place in South America. A defeat, meanwhile, would have seen them miss out. Enter substitute Mario Bolatti who with just six minutes left scrambled a winner and sent them through to the Finals.

The Manager: Diego Maradona

One of the greatest players in history, Diego Maradona took over as national coach in late 2009, despite having no real coaching experience. But it's not been easy. A 6-1 defeat to Bolivia and humiliation by Brazil in qualifying left him and his team in a precarious position but, thanks to Mario Bolatti, he can now lead his team into the Finals once more.

Key Man: Carlos Tevez

Three time South American Player of the Year, Carlos Tevez is the kind of industrious and imaginative player that every team needs. With his tireless work rate and an eye for goal, he has proved to be a key signing for his club Manchester City this year and is equally important to Argentina's chances in South Africa in 2010.

Nigeria

GROUP B

The 'Super Eagles' are flying again. But can they finally get past the last 16?

FIFA World Cup™ Record

Having qualified three time before (1994, 1998 and 2002), Nigeria know what the pressure of the FIFA World Cup™ Finals is all about. And while they have yet to get past the second round, they have come extremely close in the past. In 1994, for instance, they were within a minute of reaching the quarter-finals but a last-gasp equaliser from Italy's Roberto Baggio took the game into extra-time and they eventually lost 2-1.

FIFA World Cups™
Hosted: *0*

Best FIFA World Cup™
Finish: *Last 16 – 1994, 1998*

How They Qualified

After a tense qualification campaign where it had seemed that the pacesetters Tunisia were all set to go through, Nigeria pipped them to the post, defeating Kenya 3-2 in Nairobi in November. With Mozambique winning against Tunisia on the same night, it meant that the Super Eagles went through to the Finals.

Manager:
Shaibu Amodo

Appointed head coach in April 2008, Amodo replaced temporary coach James Peters who had taken over in the wake of Berti Vogts departure. This is his third stint in charge of the Nigerian national team, having coached them in 1996 and 2000.

Key Man: Yakubu

Strong, fearless and lethal in front of goal, Yakubu Aiyegbeni – 'the Yak' to his fans – is a powerhouse of a centre-forward. A striker for English Premiership side Everton, his goal against Kenya in November proved vital in securing Nigeria's qualification.

South Korea GROUP B

The semi-finalists from 2002 are back again, but what can we expect from the gallant South Koreans this time around?

FIFA World Cup™ Record

With the best FIFA World Cup™ record of any team in Asia, South Korea has now qualified for the last eight FIFA World Cup™ Finals, something that no other side from the continent has ever achieved. In 2002, as co-hosts with Japan, they also became the first and only team from Asia to reach the semi-finals of the FIFA World Cup™, beating the might of European football, including Italy, Portugal and Spain along the way before losing out to a single goal from Germany's Michael Ballack.

FIFA World Cups™ Hosted:
1 – 2002 (with Japan)

Best FIFA World Cup™ Finish: *4th – 2002*

How They Qualified

Despite being drawn against some of the toughest teams in Asia (Saudi Arabia, Iran, North Korea and the UAE), South Korea remained unbeaten throughout their qualifying campaign, topping their group on 16 points, four points clear of their neighbours, Korea DPR.

Key Man: Park Ji-Sung

A megastar in his own country, midfielder Park Ji-Sung has also acquired a devoted following in England where his performances for Manchester United over the past four years have not only won him many fans but seven trophies as well.

The Manager: Huh Jung-Moo

A distinguished former South Korean international, Huh Jung-Moo has also been involved with the coaching of the South Korean team for the past 20 years, either as coach, trainer or assistant manager. It's clear then that nobody knows the team – his team – better than him.

Greece

Can the Euro 2004 champions repeat their success on the world stage?

FIFA World Cups™ Hosted: *0*
Best FIFA World Cup™ Finish: *Group stages – 1994*

FIFA World Cup™ Record

Given that Greece won the 2004 European Championship in 2004, you could be forgiven that they have an equally impressive record in the FIFA World Cup™. Not so. To date, they have appeared in the FIFA World Cup™ Finals just once in their history, suffering a first round elimination in 1994 in the United States.

How They Qualified

By finishing second in UEFA Group 2 behind Switzerland, Greece secured a play-off berth against the Ukraine, a tie that would be settled by a single goal. In the second leg in Donetsk it was Dimitris Salpingidis of Panathinaikos who netted the all-important winner, taking Greece through to the Finals.

Key Man: Theofanis Gekas

A top goalscorer both in his native Greece and in Germany for Bayern Leverkusen and VfL Bochum, Gekas is one of the most reliable marksmen in European football, a fact proved when he became the leading scorer in the UEFA section of 2010 FIFA World Cup™ qualifying.

The Manager: Otto Rehhagel

As the man that steered Greece to their surprising win at Euro 2004, Rehhagel is the manager that can do no wrong. Now, having claimed qualification for the 2010 FIFA World Cup South Africa™, the former Bayern Munich coach is charged with making some new headlines for his enterprising side.

25

England

GROUP C

It's been 44 years since England won their one and only FIFA World Cup™ but after a record-breaking qualifying campaign, they arrive in South Africa full of confidence and with an expectant nation back home willing them on...

FIFA World Cups™
Hosted: *1- 1966*

FIFA World Cups™
Won: *1 – 1966*

FIFA World Cup™ Record

Since England won the FIFA World Cup™ in 1966, they have come close but never quite managed to emulate the feat of Sir Alf Ramsey's team. In 1970, they surrendered a two goal lead against West Germany, losing 3-2 in the quarter-finals, while in 1986, they were undone by the brilliance of Argentina's Diego Maradona. Four years later, they came within a whisker of the Final but lost in an agonising penalty shoot-out to Germany. Will this be their year?

How They Qualified

Rarely has an England team looked so impressive in qualifying for the Finals. With eight straight wins – including home and away victories over much-fancied Croatia – they made it to South Africa with two games to spare, scoring a record number of goals and conceding just a handful in the process.

Manager: Fabio Capello

Since he took over as England coach in December 2007 Fabio Capello's influence on the England team has been nothing short of miraculous. Far from the dispirited team that failed to qualify for EURO 2008, England breezed through their qualifying campaign and now rank as one of the favourites to win in South Africa.

Key Man: Steven Gerrard

Either wide on the right or in the middle, Steven Gerrard is a midfield maestro who can single-handedly transform a game. A tireless runner and with skill in abundance, he can split defences wide open with his laser-like passing or score the most spectacular of goals. In short, he's the perfect football machine.

USA

GROUP C

Now a regular fixture in the FIFA World Cup™ Finals and with a flourishing domestic league, it seems that the USA has finally taken football to its heart...

> **FIFA World Cups™**
> **Hosted:** *1 – 1994*
> **Best FIFA World Cup™ Finish:**
> *3rd place – 1930*

FIFA World Cup™ Record

In the inaugural FIFA World Cup™ in 1930, the USA reached the semi-finals losing 6-1 to Argentina. Famously, they also beat England in the 1950 event in Brazil. But it was 40 years until the United States re-appeared in the Finals at Italia 90. Since then they've been ever present – making the quarter-finals in 2002 – a sure sign that the team, and US soccer as a whole, is on the up.

How They Qualified

Just four points separated the top four nations in the final stage of this incredibly tight qualifying group. A 3-2 away win in Honduras in October 2009, ensured the USA qualified impressively as group winners.

The Manager: Bob Bradley

Bob Bradley boasts more victories than any other coach in Major League soccer. Since taking over since taking over from Bruce Arena after the 2006 FIFA World Cup™ Finals, he's proved himself more than capable as the national coach too.

Key Man: Landon Donovan

As the record goalscorer for his country, Landon Donovan is the undisputed superstar of American soccer. A key man in the LA Galaxy attack, Donovan is a five-time winner of the US Player of the Year award and also holds the record for the most number of assists.

Algeria

Tough, determined and organised, the 'Desert Foxes' could cause a few upsets this summer...

FIFA World Cups™ Hosted: *0*

Best FIFA World Cup™ Finish: *1st Round – 1982, 1986*

FIFA World Cup™ Record

During the golden age of Algerian football in the 1980s, the Desert Foxes qualified for both the 1982 Finals in Spain and for Mexico four years later. While they failed to make it past the group stages, the very fact that they had established themselves as a force in world football reflected the giant strides Algeria had made.

How They Qualified

A first-half wonder strike from centre half Antar Yahia gave Algeria a priceless and memorable victory against fierce rivals Egypt. The one-off/winner-takes all play-off took place on neutral ground in the Sudanese capital, Khartoum.

Key Man: Rafik Saifi

An attacking midfielder and sometime second striker, Saifi has spent much of his career in the French League, but now plays in Qatar with Al-Khor Sports Club. A veteran of the national team, he has an impressive scoring record at international level.

The Manager: Rabah Saadane

Now in his fifth spell in charge of the Algerian national team, it's safe to say Rabah Saadane knows Algerian football like no other coach. He's been here before too, having led the team in the 1986 finals in Mexico.

Slovenia

After a shock win against Russia in the play-offs, can Slovenia spring another surprise this summer...

FIFA World Cups™
Hosted: 0

Best FIFA World Cup™
Finish: 1st Round – 2002

FIFA World Cup™ Record

Prior to qualifying for the 2010 tournament, Slovenia has just one appearance in the FIFA World Cup™ Finals, when they failed to make it out of the group stages in Japan and South Korea in 2002.

How They Qualified

With one of the meanest defences in the qualification stages, Slovenia comfortably secured second spot in a group containing Slovakia, the Czech Republic, Poland Northern Ireland and San Marino. Then, in a two-legged play-off against much-fancied Russia, they beat the odds to win on away goals and book their place at the finals in the summer.

The Manager: Matjaz Kek

After guiding Maribor to back-to-back Slovenian league titles, Matjaz Kek was eventually offered the position of Slovenian national coach, via some impressive work with the Under-15 and Under-16 Slovenian teams.

Key Man: Samir Handanovic

Giant goalkeeper Samir Handanovic was one of the main reasons why Slovenia boasted such an impressive defensive record on their way to the Finals. The Udinese man conceded just four goals in their ten qualification games

Germany

One thing is certain at South Africa 2010, the German team will, as ever, be involved in the latter stages of the tournament.

FIFA World Cups™
Hosted: *2 – 1974, 2006*
FIFA World Cups™ Won:
3 – 1954, 1974, 1990

FIFA World Cup™ Record

Germany's record in the FIFA World Cup™ is exceptional. With three wins, four runners-up places and three third place finishes, they are a team who rarely fail to progress to the knock-out stages of the tournament. In the 1950s they were tough and determined. In the mid-1970s, led by Franz Beckenbauer, they reigned supreme and in 1990, with Beckenbauer now as coach, they ruled the world once more. Expect them to be just as difficult to beat this time around.

How They Qualified

It says a lot about the steel and resolve of the German national team that they secured their place in the 2010 FIFA World Cup™ Finals by winning away in Moscow, traditionally one of the hardest places for visitors to get a result. In short, they're one tough team.

Key Man: Michael Ballack

Appointed captain by former coach Jurgen Klinsmann in 2004, the Chelsea star has enjoyed an incredible international career with Germany. With almost a goal every two games from midfield, his is a record that compares favorably with most strikers. Indeed, Germany has never lost a game when Ballack has scored.

Manager: Joachim Löw

Joachim Löw has been an unexpected success as the coach of the national side since taking over from Jurgen Klinsmann after the 2006 competition. Affable, knowledgeable and tactically astute, he took Germany to the Final of the 2008 European Championships where they lost to Spain and has now led them to comfortable qualification for South Africa. Yes, the team are still as strong defensively as they have always been but now thanks to forwards like Miroslav Klose and Lucas Podolski they also have a potent attacking force as well.

Australia

After a lean spell on the international stage, Australia are finally beginning to realise their undoubted potential. Can they go far in South Africa?

FIFA World Cups™
Hosted: *0*
Best FIFA World Cup™
Finish: *Last 16 – 2006*

FIFA World Cup™ Record

Australia made their debut appearance in the FIFA World Cup™ in 1974, impressing everyone with their resilience and team spirit, even though they returned home after the first round. It would be 32 years however, until Australia returned to the FIFA World Cup™ Finals when they were unlucky to lose to eventual champions Italy by a single goal.

How They Qualified

Australia emerged from a tough group that included Qatar, Iraq and China, in the initial stages of Asian qualifying. They booked their place in South Africa with a goalless draw in Doha against Qatar in June 2009, and eventually finished top of Group A by five clear points.

Key Man: Tim Cahill

An attacking midfielder with English Premier League side Everton, Cahill is the kind of industrious player who never stops running. With a goal every two games for Australia, he's sure to be one of the main goal threats for the Socceroos come this summer.

Manager: Pim Verbeek

Verbeek took charge of the Socceroos in December 2007. He certainly has invaluable FIFA World Cup™ experience. In 2002, he was Guus Hiddink's assistant with South Korea, helping them to the semi-finals, and four years later he was Dick Advocaat's number two as the South Koreans once again impressed in the Finals.

31

Serbia

Tough, skilful and athletic, Will this be the year where Serbia fulfil their undoubted potenital?

FIFA World Cups™
Hosted: *0*
Best FIFA World Cups™
Finish: *1st round – 2006*
(as Serbia & Montenegro)

FIFA World Cup™ Record

This will be Serbia's first major tournament in its own right. They did participate in 2006 as Serbia & Montenegro After an undefeated qualifying campaign, they then lost all of their three group games and were eliminated after the first round.

How They Qualified

In their first ever qualifying campaign as an independent nation Serbia impressively topped their qualifying group, leaving the group favourites and 2006 finalists France to battle it out in the play-offs.

Manager:
Radomir Antic

After a four year break from coaching, Antic accepted the position of Serbia coach in August 2008. Having coached at giants like Real Madrid, Atletico Madrid and Barcelona, he certainly has the managerial pedigree to suggest that his team could be one of the surprise packages of the tournament.

Key Man:
Nemanja Vidic

A tower of strength for Manchester United in the English Premier League, Nemanja Vidic is one of the toughest players around, possessing all the attributes you would expect from one of the world's most accomplished defenders. Uncompromising, fearless and rarely ruffled, he was an integral part of the so-called "Famous Four" defence that conceded just a single goal in qualifying for the 2006 FIFA World Cup™ Finals.

Ghana

The "Black Stars" are known for the physical presence and never-say-die spirit. In short, they're one team you don't want to be drawn against...

FIFA World Cups™
Hosted: *0*

Best FIFA World Cup™
Finish: *Last 16 – 2006*

FIFA World Cup™ Record

Like many of the African nations, Ghana is now benefitting from having many of its players plying their trade in the strongest leagues in world football. The result is a team packed with stars. From to Michael Essien to Sulley Muntari, Hans Sarpei to Asamoah Gyan, the Ghanaian squad has sparkling talent and real strength in depth. This time they'll be hoping to improve on their debut appearance in 2006, when they reached the second round.

How They Qualified

The "Black Stars" booked their place at the Finals – their second successive appearance – after a 2-0 win in Accra against Sudan. Qualifying with two games to spare, they emerged from a group that also included Mali and Benin.

Key Man: Michael Essien

The man they call "The Bison" is not just one of the central characters in Chelsea's Premiership challenge, but the driving force behind Ghana's emergence as one of the strongest African nations. A defensive midfielder, he's one of the world's best tacklers and his high-tempo style guarantees the opposition have little time on the ball.

The Manager: Milovan Rajevac

Serbian coach Milovan Rajevac was appointed as coach of Ghana in August 2008, following in the footsteps of the interim manager Selleh Tetteh. A former manager of Red Star Belgrade, he also turned Serbia's FK Borac from relegation strugglers into UEFA Cup contenders.

33

Netherlands

It's one of football's great mysteries why the Dutch have never won a FIFA World Cup™. But with a seemingly never-ending line of talented players coming through you can bet that they'll be looking to reach the later stages of the tournament...

FIFA World Cup™ Record

The Netherland's FIFA World Cup™ history is a story of what might have been. In the 1970s, they were arguably the best team on the planet and their brand of so-called "Total Football" as characterised by Johan Cruyff was envied the world over. They reached successive Finals in 1974 and 1978 but lost both to the host nations, Germany and Argentina respectively. Since the glory days of the 1970s, though, The Netherlands have failed to reach another Final. The closest they came was the semi-finals at France 1998 when they lost on penalties to Brazil.

> FIFA World Cups™
> Hosted: *0*
>
> Best FIFA World Cup™
> Finish: *2nd – 1974, 1978*

How They Qualified

Drawn in a group with Norway, Scotland, Macedonia and Iceland Holland became the first European qualifiers when they defeated Iceland 2-1 in June 2009. Like England, the Dutch also won eight straight games to qualify, finishing their group with a 100 per cent record and conceding just two goals in the entire campaign.

Manager:
Bert van Marwijk

Although he only won a single cap for the Dutch national side, Bert van Marwijk certainly knows his football. A successful club manger with the likes of Feyernoord, Borussia Dortmund and Fortuna Sittard, he succeeded Marco van Basten as coach and despite some initial doubts from the fans he has silenced his critics by leading the Netherlands to a faultless qualification campaign.

Key Man:
Klaas Jan Huntelaar

The all-time top scorer of the Dutch Under-21 team with 18 goals in just 22 games, Huntelaar is a striker in the mould of Dutch masters like Marco van Basten and Ruud van Nistelrooy. Now 26, he has matured into a goalscorer of rare quality and following a €15 million move in the summer of 2009 he now plays his club football for Italian giants AC Milan.

Denmark

After a surprisingly successful qualifying campaign, Denmark have stormed into the Finals and look well placed to have their most successful FIFA World Cup™ to date...

FIFA World Cup™ Record

Given Scandinavia's obsession with soccer, it's a little surprising that Denmark only qualified for its first FIFA World Cup™ Finals in 1986 where they made the last 16 in Mexico. Since then, they have reached the quarter-finals in France 1998, losing narrowly to Brazil 3-2 and the last 16 four years later in Japan and South Korea.

**FIFA World Cups™
Hosted:** *0*

Best FIFA World Cup™ Finish:
Quarter-finals – 1986, 1998

How They Qualified

Faced with a difficult group including Portugal, Sweden and Hungary, Denmark booked their place with a 1-0 win over near-neighbours Sweden in Copenhagen in October 2009. With just one defeat and just five goals conceded in their ten qualifying games, the Danes will certainly take some beating in South Africa.

Manager: Morten Olsen

In the summer of 2010, it will be ten years since Morten Olsen took over as the coach of the Danish national side. In that time, he has succeeded in making the Danes one of the most difficult nations to play against. They are tight, organised and, as many teams will find this summer, very difficult to break down.

Key Man: Nicklas Bendtner

Having made his international debut at the age of just 18, Arsenal's Nicklas Bendtner has matured into a striker of genuine class. Still only 21, he now averages a goal every three games for his country and looks set for a long and illustrious career.

Japan

Japanese football has never been bigger. With an increasingly strong domestic league, super passionate fans and a national team to be proud of, you can be sure they'll give everything in 2010.

FIFA World Cup™ Record

Japan made their first appearance in the FIFA World Cup™ Finals in France 1998 and, while they returned without a point from their three games, it proved to be a turning point for the international team. Fast-forward four years, and as co-hosts of the tournament they managed to make the last 16, eventually going out to Turkey in a narrow 1-0 defeat.

FIFA World Cups™
Hosted: *1 – 2002*

Best FIFA
World Cup™
Finish: *Last 16 – 2002*

How They Qualified:

As in 2006, Japan was the first team in the world to qualify for the Finals, beating Uzbekistan 1-0 in the fourth round of the Asian qualifiers to progress to South Africa.

Manager: Takeshi Okada

Okada is now in his second stint as the manager of the Japanese national side, having been reappointed as coach in 2007. Capped 24 times by his country, Okada was also named the Japanese Manager of the Year in 2003 and 2004 after guiding Yokohama F Marinos to successive J League titles.

Key Man: Shunsuke Nakamura

A free-kick specialist, Nakamura is a free-scoring attacking midfielder with a clutch of honours already under his belt. He won the Asian Cup in 2000 and 2004 with Japan and was named the Most Valuable Player in the latter competition. He also won six trophies in his three years in Scotland with Celtic. He has recently moved to Spain to join Espanyol.

Cameroon

After missing out in 2006, Africa's most successful FIFA World Cup™ team return to action in South Africa...

FIFA World Cups™ Hosted: *0*
Best FIFA World Cup™ Finish: *Quarter-finals – 1990*

FIFA World Cup™ Record

When it comes to the FIFA World Cup™ Finals, Cameroon stand head and shoulders above every other African nation, having qualified on five previous occasions. Moreover, they were also the first African team to reach the last eight of the competition when they were finally beaten by England 3-2 after extra-time in 1990.

How They Qualified

At times during the qualifying campaign it had seemed though Cameroon was destined to miss out on the 2010 tournament. But after a shaky start – they lost to Togo and drew with Morocco – the 'Indomitable Lions' beat Morocco 2-0 in Fez in November. Togo's win over Gabon the same night gave Cameroon their passport to their sixth Finals.

The Manager: Paul Le Guen

Former Paris St. Germain and Glasgow Rangers coach Le Guen took over the job as national team coach in July 2009 and made an immediate impact by leading Cameroon to the finals in South Africa. It was a notable achievement, not least for the fact that the so-called 'Indomitable Lions' had only one point to show from their first two games.

Key Man: Samuel Eto'o

One of the great players in world football, Eto'o was the spearhead of the all-conquering Barcelona side of recent years but now plays in Italy with Inter Milan. He is the record goalscorer in the African Cup of Nations and made his debut for his country aged just 14 in 1996. This will be his third FIFA World Cup™ finals appearance.

Italy

With four FIFA World Cup™ titles – just one fewer than Brazil – Italy have proved time and time again that they are at their best when the pressure is on…

> FIFA World Cups™
> Hosted: *2 – 1934, 1990*
> FIFA World Cups™ Won:
> *4 – 1934, 1938, 1982, 2006*

FIFA World Cup™ Record

Four-times champions and two-time runners-up, there are few teams in the world who can boast the same kind of FIFA World Cup™ heritage as Italy. Back-to-back winners in 1934 and 1938, they also took the title in 1982 beating West Germany in Spain. Four years ago, they famously defeated France on penalties in an epic final in Berlin's Olympiastadion.

How They Qualified

Drawn in Group Eight alongside the Republic of Ireland, Bulgaria, Cyprus, Montenegro and Georgia, it seemed as though the Azzurri would have a fairly trouble-free route to South Africa. And so it proved, as a last gasp Alberto Gilardino goal against the Republic of Ireland in October secured a 2-2 draw and a place in the Finals.

The Manager: Marcello Lippi

Now in his second stint in charge of the Azzuri, Lippi has a reputation for being one of the best man managers in football placing a heavy emphasis on team spirit and a strong work ethic. Certainly, it's a policy that has paid dividends. In his career he has won five Italian Serie A titles, the UEFA Champions League and, of course, the FIFA World Cup™ with Italy in 2006.

Key Man: Gianluigi Buffon

The most expensive goalkeeper in the history of the game, Juventus's Gianluigi Buffon has been central to Italy's success in recent years especially in their triumph in 2006. Quick to react, agile and fearless, he is, quite simply, the greatest keeper in the world today.

Paraguay

Paraguay remain one of the most under-rated teams in South American. But after recent wins against Brazil and Argentina, all that looks set to change...

FIFA World Cups™
Hosted: *0*
Best FIFA World Cup™
Finish: *Last 16 – 1986, 1998, 2002*

FIFA World Cup™ Record

As one of the teams that played in the inaugural FIFA World Cup™ in 1930, Paraguay has a long and rich association with the tournament, appearing in seven Finals to date. Now ranked in the top 25 teams in the world, they are one of the most consistent performers in recent FIFA World Cup™ history. If they can finally make it past the second round, they could have a major say in the competition.

How They Qualified

Paraguay made it four Finals in a row in September 2009 when they defeated Argentina 1-0 in Asuncion. They were the only team to inflict a defeat on the other automatic qualifiers from South America, Brazil.

The Manager: Gerardo Martino

A former Argentine international, Martino took over from Anibal "Mano" Ruiz in February 2007. He was chosen on the strength of his record in Paraguay's domestic league where he was won titles with both Club Libertad and Cerro Porteno.

Key Man: Claudio Morel Rodriguez

While most people associate South American players with flair and attacking prowess, there are some defenders, like Claudio Morel Rodriguez, who deserve their share of the limelight. Now at Boca Juniors in Argentina, this lively left-back was voted Paraguayan Footballer of the Year in 2008.

New Zealand

For so long overshadowed by their rugby union counterparts, the All Blacks, has the time finally arrived for the All Whites to make a name for themselves?

FIFA World Cups™
Hosted: *0*
Best FIFA World Cup™
Finish: *1st round – 1982*

FIFA World Cup™ Record

With rugby the national sport and with more sheep in the country than there are people, it's hardly surprising that New Zealand often struggle to qualify for the Finals. To date, they've only appeared once, in Spain in 1982, where they lost all of their three group games to Scotland, the USSR and to Brazil.

How They Qualified

Having topped the group in the second round of Oceania qualifying, the Kiwis advanced to a play-off against Bahrain. After a goalless draw in Manama the All Whites ensured their place in the finals with a narrow 1-0 win in the return leg. A record 35,194 fans packed the stadium in Wellington in November – the biggest crowd to ever watch a game of soccer in the country.

Key Man: Shane Smeltz

The Oceania Player of the Year in 2007, Smeltz is the focal point for all of New Zealand's attacks. A prolific goalscorer at club level – he once scored 26 goals in 50 games for England's AFC Wimbledon – he also boasts an impressive goalscoring ratio of around one goal every two games at international level.

Manager: Ricki Herbert

As a player, national team coach Ricki Herbert won over 60 caps for the All Whites in the 1980s, including the games at the 1982 FIFA World Cup™ Finals in Spain. The New Zealand Coach of the Year in 2007, Herbert also combines his job with his role of manager at club side Wellington Phoenix.

Slovakia

GROUP F

A debut appearance in a major tournament Finals awaits this gifted generation of players...

FIFA World Cups™ Hosted: *0*
Best FIFA World Cups™ Finish: *2nd place – 1962 (as Czechoslovakia)*

FIFA World Cup™ Record

While it was still part of Czechoslovakia, the team actually reached the Final of the 1962 tournament, losing out 3-1 to Brazil in Santiago. Now, as Slovakia, they are preparing for their first appearance in a major Finals.

How They Qualified

Emerging from the tight Group Three in which any number of teams could have qualified, Slovakia earned their place in the Finals after a 1-0 win away in snowy Poland. The result ensured they topped their group ahead of Slovenia, the Czech Republic, Northern Ireland and Poland.

The Manager: Vladimir Weiss

Having played for the Czechoslovakia team that reached the quarter-finals of the 1990 FIFA World Cup™ in Italy, Weiss, unlike his squad, has vital first hand experience of the world's biggest sporting event. It may prove invaluable.

Key Man: Martin Skrtel

The two-time Slovak Player of the Year is an integral part of coach Weiss's plans. Tall, deceptively quick and with a commanding presence in the air, he is now replicating his outstanding displays for his club Liverpool for his country as well.

Brazil

Where do you start with Brazil? Quite simply they remain the benchmark for all other international teams...

FIFA World Cups™ Hosted: *1950*

FIFA World Cups™ Won: *5 – 1958, 1962, 1970, 1994, 2002*

FIFA World Cup™ Record

No other team in the history of the FIFA World Cup™ has achieved as much as Brazil. Five times winners and twice runners-up they have always been the team to fear at the Finals. From the golden era of the great Pelé in the late 1950s, 1960s and early 1970s to the flamboyant sides of the 1980s and 1990s, they have always played the only way they know how. That is, with skill, flair and a passion for attacking.

How They Qualified

Despite a lone defeat against Paraguay, Brazil progressed to the Finals after a 3-1 win over arch rivals Argentina in Rosario. They remain the only team to have played in the Finals of all of the FIFA World Cups™ to date.

Key Man: Kaká

Briefly the most expensive player in the world when he moved from Milan to Real Madrid in the summer of 2009 in a staggering €70 million deal, Kaká is the creative lynchpin of the Brazilian team. The FIFA World Player of the Year in 2007, he can make and score goals and he is sure to be one of the stars of the show in South Africa.

The Manager: Dunga

It says a lot about the reputation of a man that he can be appointed as the national coach without any prior coaching experience. Such is the legend of Dunga. A distinguished player with 91 caps to his credit, he captained his country to victory in the 1994 FIFA World Cup™ in the USA and has already led Brazil to a Copa America triumph and the 2009 Confederations Cup. He's added some defensive steel too, making Brazil an even more frightening prospect.

North Korea

GROUP G

It's been 44 years since North Korea appeared at the biggest tournament on the planet, so just how will they cope?

FIFA World Cups™ Hosted: *0*

Best FIFA World Cup™ Finish: *Second round – 1966*

FIFA World Cup™ Record

The North Koreans may have only ever qualified for one FIFA World Cup™ Finals in their history but what a tournament it was. Rewind to England in 1966 and the little-known North Koreans arrived as the underdogs of the tournament. What happened next though was barely believable. Against all the odds, they beat the might of Italy and qualified for the next phase. Then, against Portugal they were 3-0 up after just 25 minutes but fell apart, leaving the legendary Eusebio to claw his team back into the game with four goals to give them a famous 5-3 victory.

How They Qualified

North Korea had to enter the qualifying campaign in the very first round of the Asian competition. Following wins against Mongolia and Jordan, they advanced to the group stages where they came second in a group featuring South Korean, Iran, Saudi Arabia and the UAE, pipping Saudi Arabia to the second automatic place on goal difference. This means that both North Korea and South Korea will feature in a FIFA World Cup™ Finals together for the first time.

The Manager: Kim Jong-Hun

Jong-Hun has managed to achieve great things with North Korea. His team, while lacking superstar talents, is nevertheless organised, compact and willing to give their all for the cause. They'll be difficult to beat this summer.

KeyMan: Ri Myong-guk

Every good team needs a reliable goalkeeper and they don't come much more solid than Ri Myong-guk. With four clean sheets in five games in qualifying, he was the star of the show in the 0-0 draw against Saudi Arabia in Riyadh, the game that assured his team of qualification for 2010.

Côte d'Ivoire GROUP G

With players like Didier Drogba, Emanuel Eboué and the Toure brothers, Kolo and Yaya, the Côte d'Ivoire could prove to be the surprise package of the 2010 FIFA World Cup South Africa™...

FIFA World Cups™
Hosted: 0

Best FIFA World Cup™
Finish:
1st round – 2006

FIFA World Cup™ Record

The Côte d'Ivoire only made their first appearance in the FIFA World Cup™ Finals four years ago in Germany. Unlucky to be drawn in the so-called 'Group of Death' with Argentina, the Netherlands and Serbia & Montenegro, they lost their first two games but salvaged some pride with a 3-2 victory over Serbia & Montenegro in their final game.

How They Qualified

The Côte d'Ivoire went into their final qualifying game in African Group E undefeated and needing just a draw against Malawi to make it to the Finals. A goal from substitute Didier Drogba made the score 1-1 and 'Les Elephants' duly made it through.

Key Man: Didier Drogba

As one of the star players in the FA Premier League, Didier Drogba is every defender's worst nightmare. Lightning fast, ultra-powerful and blessed with an eye for goal that has seen him score at will for Chelsea and his country, he is one of the most complete strikers in the world.

The Manager: Vahid Halilhodzic

Having led clubs such as Paris St. Germain in France and Trabzonspor in Turkey, Vahid Halilhodzic is a coach of vast experience. Manager of the Côte d'Ivoire since May 2008, he has overseen a smooth and trouble-free passage to the 2010 World Cup South Africa™ Finals. The real test, however, will come this summer.

Portugal

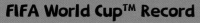

GROUP G

Undoubtedly one of the most gifted teams in European football, but have they got what it takes to take on the world this year?

FIFA World Cup™ Record

It's one of those strange football anomalies that Portugal has only been in four FIFA World Cup™ Finals in their history. That said, in two of those appearances they have reached the semi-finals, taking third place in 1966 and fourth place in the last FIFA World Cup™ in Germany in 2006.

FIFA World Cups™ Hosted: *0*
Best FIFA World Cup™ Finish: *3rd place – 1966*

The Manager: Carlos Queiroz

Not only has Carlos Queiroz managed Real Madrid but as right-hand man to Sir Alex Ferguson at Manchester United, he helped oversee one of the most successful periods in the club's history. Now, as Portuguese coach, he is charged with helping his team build on the massive progress they made under former manager Luis Felipe Scolari.

How They Qualified

Like France, Portugal made hard work of reaching South Africa. Drawn in a group with Denmark, Sweden, Hungary, Albania and Malta, they pipped the Swedes to second placed despite a poor start to the campaign and then narrowly beat Bosnia and Herzegovina in a play-off to win their place.

Key Man: Cristiano Ronaldo

The world's most expensive player, Ronaldo moved from Manchester United to Real Madrid for a jaw-dropping €94 million in the summer of 2009. Now the captain of his country, Ronaldo's incomparable skill has brought him many personal accolades, not least the FIFA World Player of the Year award in 2008.

45

Spain

The European Champions arrive in South Africa as one of the hottest favourites for the FIFA World Cup™. Will this be the year they finally deliver?

FIFA World Cups™
Hosted: *1 – 1982*
Best FIFA World Cup™
Finish: *4th – 1950*

FIFA World Cup™ Record

For a country with such a rich history in club football, Spain's failure to make any real impact at the FIFA World Cup™ Finals is truly baffling. Despite boasting such legendary names as Andoni Zubizaretta, Jose Antonio Camacho and Emilio "The Vulture" Butragueno, Spain has only one semi-final place from 12 appearances to show for their efforts. Can they go one better this time?

How They Qualifed

Like the Dutch and the English, the Spanish qualified for the Finals at a canter, winning all of their games and conceding just two goals in the process. Given that they had to contend with opposition as strong as Turkey and Bosnia and Herzigovina, that's no mean feat.

The Manager: Vincent del Bosque

It was always going to be a tough act to follow in the footsteps of Luis Aragones, but former Real Madrid coach Vincent del Bosque had made it seem simple. Of course, his job has been made easier by having one of the best squads in world football. With the likes of Fernando Torres, David Villa and Xavi all at his disposal, he really is spoilt for choice.

Key Man: Andres Iniesta

Anyone who saw Barcelona's consummate victory over Manchester United in the 2009 UEFA Champions League Final will know only too well what Andres Iniesta is capable of. A tireless and inventive attacking midfielder, United's Wayne Rooney described him as the "best player in the world". It's hard to disagree.

Switzerland GROUP H

After decades in the international wilderness, Switzerland finally look like they have a team and a manager to bring them success this summer...

FIFA World Cups™
Hosted: *1 - 1954*

Best FIFA World Cup™
Finish: *Quarter-finals
– 1934, 1938, 1954*

FIFA World Cup™ Record

Success has been thin on the ground for the Swiss in recent years. With only two appearances in the Finals in the last 40 years, where they failed, on both occasions, to get past the last 16, it's high time they delivered on the biggest stage. Maybe this will be the year.

How They Qualified

Despite a blip against Luxembourg where they lost 2-1, the Swiss topped their Group in qualifying, with home and away wins against a strong Greece team, giving them the momentum to go all the way. They wrapped up their place in the Finals with a goalless draw against Israel in Basle in October 2009.

The Manager: Ottmar Hitzfeld

With a tally of 18 major titles gleaned from coaching spells with Grasshoppers in Switzerland and Borussia Dortmund and Bayern Munich in Germany, Ottmar Hitzfeld has a record that compares with the very best managers in the game. Now, Hitzfeld is charged with bringing the same success to the Swiss side.

Key Man: Alexander Frei

As team captain and one of the most prolific strikers in international football, there's a lot of pressure on Alexander Frei. Throughout his career, he has maintained a staggering ratio of a goal every two games for his clubs. The scary prospect for defenders in the 2010 FIFA World Cup South Africa™ Finals is that his record for his country is even better.

Honduras

'Los Catrachos' are back for another crack at the game's biggest prize…

FIFA World Cups™
Hosted: *0*
Best FIFA World Cup™
Finish: *1st Round – 1982*

How They Qualified

A great start to their qualifying campaign (including a win over Mexico) looked set to count for nothing as the Hondurans stumbled. But thanks to a 1-0 win in El Salvador and Costa Rica collapsing against the USA, 'Los Catrachos' survived to claim the third qualifying spot in the region.

FIFA World Cup™ Record

The Honduran national side qualified for their first FIFA World Cup™ Finals in 1982 when they drew against Northern Ireland and the hosts Spain but then failed to beat Yugoslavia, resulting in elimination in the group stages. South Africa 2010 will be their second appearance in the finals.

Key Man: Wilson Palacios

A key man in the midfield of English Premiership side Tottenham Hotspur, Wilson Palacios has proved himself in one of the most demanding leagues in the world. As the lynchpin of the Honduran midfield, meanwhile, he is indispensible.

The Manager: Reinaldo Rueda

Having made his name in Colombian football where he coached the national team at U-17, U-20, U-21, U-23 and finally at senior level, Rueda took over as manager of Honduras in January 2007. Since then he has done well, getting the very best out of the small Central American nation's talented crop of players

Chile

Second only to Brazil in South American qualifying, Chile have proved that they have what it takes to make great strides in South Africa this summer...

FIFA World Cup™ Record

Chile have a chequered history at the FIFA World Cup™ Finals. Though they have appeared in seven Finals, including the very first competition in 1930, they have been eliminated in the first round five times and the second round once. The only success they have enjoyed was as hosts in 1962, when they finished in a creditable third place.

FIFA World Cups™
Hosted: *1 - 1962*
Best FIFA World Cup™ Finish:
3rd place – 1962

How They Qualified

Few would have expected Marcelo Bielsa's Chilean side to give Brazil a run for their money in qualifying, but with one more win and scoring just one less goal than their illustrious neighbours they have surprised everyone – maybe even themselves.

Manager: Marcelo Bielsa

Known for being one of the most thorough and innovative coaches in the game, Marcelo Bielsa took his native Argentina to the FIFA World Cup™ Finals in 2002 and to the Olympic gold medal in 2004. He also engineered Chile's first ever win over his home nation, when they defeated Argentina 1-0 in October 2008.

Key Man: Humberto Suazo

But an outstanding goalscoring record at virtually all of the clubs he has played for, Suazo seems equally at home when playing for his country. On the way to qualification for South Africa he plundered ten goals, making him the top scorer in the South American qualifying competition, one ahead of the Brazilian Luis Fabiano.

Players to Watch

Meet the stars set to shine in South Africa

Fernando Torres
Club: *Liverpool FC*
Born: *20 March 1984*

Luis Fabiano
Club: *Sevilla*
Born: *8 November 1980*

Skills on Show
One of the most exciting players in the world today, Fernando Torres has scored goals at every level of the game.

Skills on Show
Luis Fabiano's strength on the ball and accurate finishing make him a terrifying proposition for defenders.

Goals and Glory
Torres began his career with Atlético Madrid and scored 75 goals in 174 league appearances. Now with Liverpool, he marked his first season with 20 goals. He has made over 60 appearances for Spain and scored their winning goal in the Euro 2008 Final.

Goals and Glory
Luis Fabiano scored 62 goals in 84 games for Sao Paulo and he scored in the UEFA Cup Final for Sevilla. Fabiano marked his first international appearance with a goal and helped Brazil win the Copa América in 2004, and scored an international hat trick against Portugal.

Talent to Check-out
With excellent speed, a deft touch and an eye for a stunning goal, Fernando Torres will be one of the stars of South Africa 2010.

Talent to Check-out
With an incredible record of 22 international goals in 31 appearances, defenders will fear playing against Fabiano this summer.

Keiji Tamada

Club: *Nagoya Grampus*
Born: *11 April 1980*

Skills on Show

Celebrated for his dribbling skills, accurate passing and excellent free kicks, Keiji Tamada is talented attacker with the ability to break down any defence.

Goals and Glory

Tamada plays for Nagoya Grampus where he has scored 16 goals in 84 games. He was a member of the Japanese Squad that played at the 2006 FIFA World Cup™ and scored against Brazil in the first round.

Talent to Check-out

Keiji Tamada scored twice in FIFA World Cup™ qualifying and he will be looking to add to his tally of 13 international goals at this summer's tournament.

Lionel Messi

Club: *Barcelona FC*
Born: *24 June 1987*

Skills on Show

With exhilarating pace, excellent balls skills and extraordinary vision, "Leo" Messi really does appear to be destined to become one of the greats of the game.

Goals and Glory

After being spotted playing for Argentina's Newell's Old Boys's youth team, Messi moved to Barcelona. He made his debut in the 2004 and became the youngest footballer to play a Spanish league game. A constant danger to opposition defences, Messi scored an incredible 38 goals in Barca's 2009 treble-winning season. He has been an integral part of the national team since 2004 and helped Argentina win gold at the 2008 Olympics.

Talent to Check-out

All eyes will be on Messi this summer. His mesmerising skills are sure to set the tournament alight.

Players to Watch

Wayne Rooney
Club: *Manchester United*
Born: *24 October 1985*

Skills on Show
Powerful and passionate, Rooney's close control, eye for goal and his never-say-die attitude is sure to give defenders a hard time at the Finals.

Achievements
Where do you start? He may only be 24 but Rooney has already won three FA Premier League titles, a UEFA Champions League winners medal and the FIFA World Club championship as well.

Talent to Check Out
With a goal every two games for England, Rooney is sure to be one of the contenders for the Golden Boot in 2010.

Lukas Podolski
Club: *FC Koln*
Born: *4 June 1985*

Skills on Show
If the goalscoring exploits of Miroslav Klose were something to marvel at then those of Lukas Podolski seem set to eclipse him. A goal every two games for Germany have made this young striker not merely one of the first names on the team sheet but also one of the most feared strikers in Europe.

Achievements
One of the top strikers at the 2006 FIFA World Cup™ in Germany where he scored three goals, Podolski also won the Gillette Best Young Player of the Year award that year, beating Cristiano Ronaldo to the title. He is also only the second player after Gerd Muller to score four goals in a game for Germany, when he starred in the 13-0 win against San Marino in their Euro 2008 qualifier.

Talent to Check Out
Podolski has forged a terrific understanding with his striker partner Miroslav Klose. Interestingly, the duo are both Polish-born and often speak in Polish to confuse opposing defenders.

Carlos Vela

Club: *Arsenal*
Born: *1 March 1989*

Skills on Show

Arsenal striker Carlos Vela is quick witted and fleet footed and has been earmarked as one of the real stars of the future.

Achievements

Even though he's still just 20, Vela already has a great track record in international football, claiming the Golden Boot Award in Mexico's victorious 2005 FIFA World Under 17-Championship. More recently, he played pivotal role in his country's win in the 2009 CONCACAF Gold Cup over the USA.

Talent to Check Out

With an average of a goal every three games for his country, clearly Carlos Vela is a striker with an eye for goal. Expect him to be one of the shining young talents of 2010.

Asamoah Gyan

Club: *Stade Rennais*
Born: *22 November 1985*

Skills on Show

Dynamic, skilful and capable of scoring spectacular goals, expect a queue of clubs lining up to sign Asamoah Gyan once the FIFA World Cup™ Finals end.

Achievements

Gyan will forever be known as the scorer of Ghana's first ever goal in the FIFA World Cup™ Finals when he netted against the Czech Republic in 2006 after just 68 seconds. It was also the fastest goal of that tournament.

Talent to Check Out

Gyan has had a staggering start to the new season with his French club, Stade Rennais. It's a rich vein of form that he will hope to continue in the summer of 2010.

Players to Watch

Carlos Pavón
Club: *Real C.D. Espana*
Born: *9 October 1973*

Karim Benzema
Club: *Real Madrid*
Born: *19 December 1987*

Skills on Show
He may be at the tail end of his career, but there may just be one last hurrah for the veteran striker Carlos Pavón. Given half a chance, there are few strikers in the game as well-equipped to find the back of the net.

Skills on Show
He may only be 22 but he plays with the wisdom and intelligence of a more experienced striker. Strong and quick, what's frightening is that his best years are still ahead of him.

Achievements
A four-time Ligue 1 winner with his hometown club, Lyon, Benzema was the top goalscorer in the French league in 2007–08, a year which he was voted the Player of the Year. He was also a member of the French Under-17 team that won the European Championship in 2004.

Achievements
The all-time record scorer for Honduras, Pavón is also the reigning Honduran Footballer of the Year. He's also played in countries including Italy, Mexico and the USA.

Talent to Check Out
This striker has an obscene amount of talent which is why, in July 2009, Real Madrid paid €35 million for him.

Talent to Check Out
Averaging around a goal every two games, Pavón has proved that he has what it takes at international level.

Sekou Cissé

Club: *Feyenoord*
Born: *23 May 1985*

Simaõ Sabrosa

Club: *Atletico Madrid*
Born: *31 October 1979*

Skills on Show
A striker that's equally adept at drifting out wide and providing assists, Cissé is, like many of his team-mates, fast, skilful and extremely athletic.

Skills on Show
A fans' favourite, Simaõ is a pacy winger who loves to run at defenders and provide the ammunition for his strikers. Quick, agile and blessed with exquisite dribbling skills, he's sure to make an impact this summer.

Achievements
The top scorer at the 2008 Toulon tournament for Under-23 sides, Cissé was also a member of the Ivory Coast Olympic team and recently moved to Dutch giants Feyernoord in a five-year deal.

Achievements
A member of the Portugal team that came second in Euro 2004 and the side that reached the semi-finals of the 2006 FIFA World Cup™, Simaõ has also won the Portuguese Liga, Super Cup and Portuguese Cup with Benfica. In 2007 he was voted Portuguese Player of the Year.

Talent to Check Out
Cissé's main weapon is his pace. Couple that with an eye for goal and a strike partner as talented at Didier Drogba, and you have, potentially, one of the most dangerous forward lines at the 2010 FIFA World Cup™.

Talent to Check Out
Pace? Check. Ball control? Check? Dead ball ability? Check. Yes, Simaõ has got the lot and he's also coolness personified when it comes to penalty shoot-outs.

FIFA World Cup™ in Numbers

At the FIFA World Cup™ there's more to numbers than just the final score...

25
The number of FIFA World Cup™ Finals appearances made by Germany's Lothar Matthäus over five tournaments.

365
The height in millimeters of the FIFA World Cup™ trophy itself.

24
The number of passes completed by the Argentina team before midfielder Esteban Cambiasso scored against Serbia & Montenegro in 2006. It was voted Goal of the Tournament.

162
The height in centimeters of Ecuador's Christian Lara – the shortest player in the 2006 FIFA World Cup™ in Germany.

113

The minute in which Laurent Blanc scored the first ever "golden goal" in FIFA World Cup™ history for France against Paraguay in 1998.

26.29 billion

The estimated total cumulative worldwide television audience during the entire 2006 FIFA World Cup™ tournament in Germany.

3

The number of penalty shoot-outs lost by both Italy and England in FIFA World Cup™ history.

42

Striker Roger Milla's age when he represented Cameroon in the 1994 FIFA World Cup™ in the USA.

11

The number of teams that have appeared in a FIFA World Cup™ Final: Brazil, Italy, West Germany, Argentina, Uruguay, France and England have all won at least one title, The Netherlands, Czechoslovakia, Hungary and Sweden are all losing finalists.

13

The record number of goals in a single FIFA World Cup™ – scored by France's Just Fontaine in 1958.

Puzzles & Games

FIFA World Cup™ Legends Wordsearch

Hidden in the grid opposite you will find the surnames of 25 FIFA World Cup™ legends from the past 50 years. All the names are in a straight line, but they may be forwards or backwards, up or down, or even diagonally. How long will it take you to find them all?

GORDON **BANKS**

FRANZ **BECKENBAUER**

DAVID **BECKHAM**

JOHAN **CRUYFF**

EUSEBIO

GEOFF **HURST**

MARIO **KEMPES**

GARY **LINEKER**

PAOLO **MALDINI**

DIEGO **MARADONA**

LOTHAR **MATTHAUS**

BENNI **MCCARTHY**

BOBBY **MOORE**

ROGER **MILLA**

GERD **MULLER**

HIDETOSHI **NAKATA**

PELE

MICHEL **PLATINI**

RONALDO

PAOLO **ROSSI**

LEONEL **SANCHEZ**

BERTI **VOGTS**

LEV **YASHIN**

ZINEDINE **ZIDANE**

PASCAL **ZUBERBUHLER**

```
V O G T S D N Z A F F Y U R C T H
H A D O N R N U K E M P E S J U N
I H O P D A L B B E K K S H R S I
D A L L I M E E N B M O O S E T N
E G B A L N D R A L G E T H N O I
U R E T B E C B K I E P G C I E D
S S C I A G D U A K N L E S H T L
A M K N S U A H T T A M E S S F A
N C H I S S Q L A E D N U P A D M
O C A X K F O E E X I E M L Y A X
D A M A N I D R R B Z C D R L D A
A R O N A L D O W W F E M D F E Q
R T O R B O K E U S E B I O C I R
A H R J L S B E C K E N B A U E R
M Y E R E K E N I L Z E H C N A S
```

SOUTH
AFRICA
2010

SOLUTION
ON PAGE 61

Puzzles & Games

Spot the Ball

The ball has been magically removed from this picture. Mark the square where you think the ball should be with an X, then check if you're right on the page opposite.

E
D
C
B
A

1 2 3 4 5 6 7

© 2007 FIFA TM

Guess Who?

Can you name these four players, from Brazil, Germany, Ghana and Argentina, who will be in South Africa in 2010?

1

2

3

4

Spot the Difference

The picture on the right has five differences from the one on the left. Can you spot them?

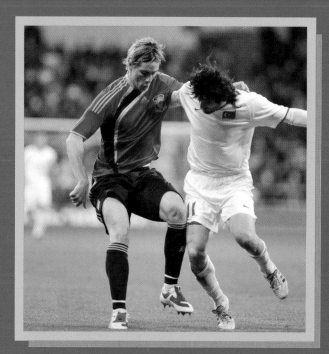

Answers

FIFA World Cup™ Legends Wordsearch from page 59.

```
V O G T S D N Z A F F Y U R C T H
H A D O N R N U K E M P E S J U N
I H O P D A L B B E K K S H R S I
D A L L I M E E N B M O O S E T N
E G B A L N D R A L G E T H N O I
U R E T B E C B K I E P G C I E D
S S C I A G D U A K N L E S H T L
A M K N S U A H T T A M E S S F A
N C H I S S Q L A E D N U P A D M
O C A X K F O E E X I E M L Y A X
D A M A N I D R R B Z C D R L D A
A R O N A L D O W W F E M D F E Q
R T O R B O K E U S E B I O C I R
A H R J L S B E C K E N B A U E R
M Y E R E K E N I L Z E H C N A S
```

Spot the Ball

E2

Guess Who?

1. Kaká; 2. Michael Ballack; 3. Michael Essien; 4. Lionel Messi.

Spot the Difference

1. FIFA World Cup™ arm badge 2. Left player's shirt number 3. Right player's shirt number 4. Sock badge 5. Ball position

61

FIFA World Cup South Africa™ Progress Chart

Group A

Date	Home		Away	Venue
11 June 2010	South Africa		Mexico	Johannesburg (S)
11 June 2010	Uruguay		France	Cape Town
16 June 2010	South Africa		Uruguay	Pretoria
17 June 2010	France		Mexico	Polokwane
22 June 2010	Mexico		Uruguay	Rustenburg
22 June 2010	France		South Africa	Bloemfontein

Team	P	W	D	L	GD	P

Group B

Date	Home		Away	Venue
12 June 2010	Argentina		Nigeria	Johannesburg (E)
12 June 2010	South Korea		Greece	Port Elizabeth
17 June 2010	Greece		Nigeria	Bloemfontein
17 June 2010	Argentina		South Korea	Johannesburg (S)
22 June 2010	Nigeria		South Korea	Durban
22 June 2010	Greece		Argentina	Polokwane

Team	P	W	D	L	GD	P

Group C

Date	Home		Away	Venue
12 June 2010	England		USA	Rustenburg
13 June 2010	Algeria		Slovenia	Polokwane
18 June 2010	Slovenia		USA	Johannesburg (E)
18 June 2010	England		Algeria	Cape Town
23 June 2010	Slovenia		England	Port Elizabeth
23 June 2010	USA		Algeria	Pretoria

Team	P	W	D	L	GD	P

Group D

Date	Home		Away	Venue
13 June 2010	Germany		Australia	Durban
13 June 2010	Serbia		Ghana	Pretoria
18 June 2010	Germany		Serbia	Port Elizabeth
19 June 2010	Ghana		Australia	Rustenburg
23 June 2010	Ghana		Germany	Johannesburg (S)
23 June 2010	Australia		Serbia	Nelspruit

Team	P	W	D	L	GD	P

Group E

Date	Home		Away	Venue
14 June 2010	Netherlands		Denmark	Johannesburg (S)
14 June 2010	Japan		Cameroon	Bloemfontein
19 June 2010	Netherlands		Japan	Durban
19 June 2010	Cameroon		Denmark	Pretoria
24 June 2010	Denmark		Japan	Rustenburg
24 June 2010	Cameroon		Netherlands	Cape Town

Team	P	W	D	L	GD	P

Group F

Date	Home		Away	Venue
14 June 2010	Italy		Paraguay	Cape Town
15 June 2010	New Zealand		Slovakia	Rustenburg
20 June 2010	Slovakia		Paraguay	Bloemfontein
20 June 2010	Italy		New Zealand	Nelspruit
24 June 2010	Slovakia		Italy	Johannesburg (E)
24 June 2010	Paraguay		New Zealand	Polokwane

Team	P	W	D	L	GD	P

Group G

Date	Home		Away	Venue
15 June 2010	Côte d'Ivoire		Portugal	Port Elizabeth
15 June 2010	Brazil		North Korea	Johannesburg (E)
20 June 2010	Brazil		Côte d'Ivoire	Johannesburg (S)
21 June 2010	Portugal		North Korea	Cape Town
25 June 2010	Portugal		Brazil	Durban
25 June 2010	North Korea		Côte d'Ivoire	Nelspruit

Team	P	W	D	L	GD	P

Group H

Date	Home		Away	Venue
16 June 2010	Honduras		Chile	Nelspruit
16 June 2010	Spain		Switzerland	Durban
21 June 2010	Chile		Switzerland	Port Elizabeth
21 June 2010	Spain		Honduras	Johannesburg (E)
25 June 2010	Chile		Spain	Pretoria
25 June 2010	Switzerland		Honduras	Bloemfontein

Team	P	W	D	L	GD	P